**Coliola, Courageous COVID Canine**

Story by Candi Werenka

Illustrations by Bethany Harris

Text copyright © 2021 by Candi Werenka/Coliola Books

Illustrations copyright © 2021 by Bethany Harris

All rights reserved. Reproduction in part or in whole is strictly forbidden without the express written consent of the publisher, with the exception of a brief quotation for review purposes.

Covers and interior layout by Orand Werenka

Scripture taken from the New King James Version ®. Copyright © 1982 by Thomas Nelson. Used by permission. All rights reserved.

ISBN: 9798701685978

This book is dedicated to Valerie Patz, a courageous lady who went to sleep battling COVID-19 and pneumonia and woke up in the presence of her Heavenly Father on November 27, 2020. May God's grace shine upon her family, just as He mirrored His grace to me when I was a young person.

# Forward

Ever since a virus called COVID-19 appeared, our world has changed a lot. Do you know what a **virus** is? It is like a cold or flu, and it makes some people very sick. This is why we must try to keep everyone around us safe. We must wear masks, sanitize our hands, and play with our friends differently—something grown-ups call **social distancing**. We can help other people by having a good attitude about these changes. We can be extra kind to our families and friends. Sometimes, change is difficult. But we must try our best not to be afraid. We must be courageous.

# 1
# A New Pet

Has your family ever decided to get a pet? Since the COVID-19 virus entered our world, many families have been spending more time at home. This makes it the perfect time for a new pet. Our pets live with us, so they must follow all the safety rules.

They must learn to be courageous, just like a floppy-eared little puppy named Coliola.

What kind of pet do you have?

Can you spot your pet in the picture?

# 2
# Welcome Coliola

Coliola was born on February 24, 2020, in Calgary, Alberta. Her two human sisters, Kelcey and Emily, took good care of her. They thought she was a courageous little puppy right from the start.

Coliola's mom Kansas is a black Labrador retriever. Her dad Charlie is a golden retriever. Coliola has brown eyes and black fur like her mom. Her fur is fluffy and her ears are floppy like her dad's.

Do you look like your mom? Or do you look more like your dad?

You are a perfect combination of your parents because you are fearfully and wonderfully made. God made you special!

# 3
# Coliola's Family

Coliola has nine brothers and sisters: Cariad, Harvey, Indy, Jasper, Keeper, Olive, Paisley, Rosie, and Shiloh.

That is a lot of brothers and sisters! How many do you have? It is nice to have our brothers and sisters to play with.

Can you spot Coliola and her brothers and sisters all tucked in and ready for bed?

How many golden puppies can you count? How many black puppies can you count?

# 4
# A New Home

Coliola went to live with her adoptive family when she was eight weeks old. Do you know what **adoptive** means? It means that sometimes kids and pets get to be loved by another family.

It took a lot of courage for Coliola to leave her nine brothers and sisters, but she is happy to be loved by her three human brothers, Oakley, Orand, and Olson.

Coliola's brothers take good care of her. They give her baths and feed her healthy food and treats.

Are you thankful for all the grocery and pet store workers who make sure we have enough food and treats during this time?

Can you spot the treats in the pet store?

# 5
# Coliola Loves Her Neighbors

Coliola is happy with her big yard and new neighbors. Her best friend is an American Staffordshire terrier named Forrest. He and Coliola play and run through the fields together.

Sometimes they even visit each other without their human families.

Did you know that it is good to love your neighbor as much as you love yourself? It is important to love others during this time, because social distancing makes many people feel lonely.

Can you spot the cookies Coliola and her family made for Forrest?

# 6
# Coliola is a Gardener

The best part about a big yard and new neighbors is sharing a garden. Coliola loves her garden. She helps plant and harvest all the fruits and vegetables. Fresh fruits and vegetables help keep your body healthy.

A lot of families have planted gardens during this time. Did your family plant a garden? Gardening is a good way to work together and share with others.

Can you guess what Coliola's favorite vegetable is?

What is your favorite vegetable?

# 7
# Coliola Visits the Veterinarian

Coliola stays healthy by eating fresh fruits and vegetables, but she must still visit her doctor for check-ups. A doctor for pets is called a **veterinarian**.

Coliola's family is not allowed to go into the veterinarian's office with her because of the COVID-19 virus. Veterinarians want to keep their furry friends safe.

Coliola's family must wait in their truck while she has her check-ups. It takes a lot of courage for Coliola to visit the veterinarian by herself, but she has a good attitude. She knows it is important to get check-ups.

Are you thankful for your doctor who helps you when you are sick and works hard to keep you safe?

Can you count the bones on Coliola's mask?

# 8
# Coliola Goes Hiking

Coliola's veterinarian says that exercise is important for both puppies and humans. Coliola is happy because she loves to hike. Have you ever been hiking?

It is a fun family activity to do while you are social distancing. The sunlight and fresh air make you stronger, so you will not get sick as easily.

It takes courage to try something new, but if you try hiking, you will see some interesting things. You might also meet some friends along the way, just like Coliola does.

Can you help Coliola find her way up Mount Indefatigable? Can you say Indefatigable?

Indefatigable means not being tired. Do you think Coliola gets tired after climbing such big mountains?

# 9
# School for Coliola

Coliola was excited to go hiking, but she was even more excited for school! She was sad when all the puppy schools closed because of the COVID-19 virus. Were you sad when your school closed?

Coliola's family took her to the dog park so she could play with other puppies. She was happy that her family helped her to be safe and meet new friends.

It is nice that your parents and teachers are trying to find ways for you to be safe. Now you can go back to school to learn and be with your friends.

Can you spot Coliola playing with her friends at the dog park in Cochrane, Alberta?

# 10
# Coliola Helps at Home

Since Coliola is not able to go to school, she works at home with her family. She learns a lot of new things at home, just like you do at school.

Sometimes she helps her dad fix things in the house. She also helps her mom cook and clean.

Because of the COVID-19 virus, a lot of parents have been working from home.

Sometimes this takes courage, but it is nice that families get to spend more time together. They can work on special projects, like building tree forts and dog houses.

Can you guess Coliola's favorite way to help at home? What is your favorite way to help at home?

# 11
# Coliola is Courageous

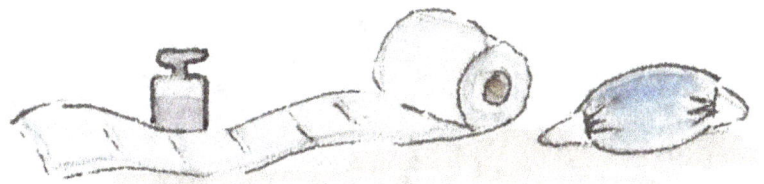

Coliola is still learning about all the changes in our world since the COVID-19 virus appeared.

Coliola knows that it is good for people to wear masks, wash and sanitize their hands, and not get too close to each other. She tries to have a good attitude every day.

Coliola wants you to pray for people who are not feeling well. She thanks God for our awesome world, loving families, healthy bodies, and our courageous COVID pets.

You can be courageous, too. Afterall, courage is contagious.... in a good way!

Can you think of ways to be kind and courageous?

"Have I not commanded you? Be strong and of good courage; do not be afraid, nor be dismayed, for the Lord your God is with you wherever you go."

Joshua 1:9

## Acknowledgements

A big hug to all whose lives have been touched by COVID-19—to our courageous health care workers, teachers, clergy, grocery and pet store owners, neighbors, and all those who put themselves on the front line every day.

Thank you to my husband Brad, my sons Oakley, Orand, and Olson, and my courageous COVID canine, Coliola, for your support and inspiration.

Thanks also to my editor, Laura Swart. Laura is a novelist, poet, and playwright and the director of I-AM ESL, an online language school that uses story and song to teach English to refugees. Visit www.iam-esl.org for details.

I am blessed by my son, Orand Werenka, an aspiring graphic and website designer, who graciously devoted his time and talents to the formatting, design, and completion of this book. Inquiries of Orand can be made at owerenka@outlook.com.

I am grateful to Hoon Kim, an innovative photographer from Calgary, Alberta. His design agency, Clarity Visual Company, offers web design, photography, videography, graphic design, and other visual arts services. Connect with Hoon at hoonkim@clarityvisual.com.

Author Candi Werenka lives in Calgary, Alberta with her husband Brad, three sons Oakley, Orand and Olson, and canine daughter Coliola. She enjoys homesteading, hiking, and PraiseMoves, a Christian alternative to yoga. She loves making others happy with homemade cards, nutritious canned goods from her garden, and educational stories for children. This is her first book in the Tails of Coliola series.

Illustrator Bethany Harris' *(BA,* University of Waterloo) paintings have received numerous awards locally and nationally. Bethany's love for God and His creation are at the heart of her energetic and captivating illustrations. She lives on a small farm in southern Alberta, where she paints, raises a flock of wooly sheep, gardens, and hikes with her dogs.

Coliola and her nine canine siblings with Kelcey Moore, Tyler Pecsi, Emily Moore, and Mike Moore.

www.ingramcontent.com/pod-product-compliance
Lightning Source LLC
Chambersburg PA
CBHW072210100526
44589CB00015B/2458